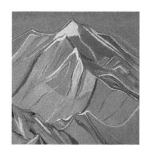

DOING ALL THE GOOD YOU CAN DAILY

31 Days of Phyllis' Success Predictors and Possibilities

PHYLLIS POTTINGER
and CAMILLE WHITEHORN

ISBN 978-1-0980-9587-1 (paperback)
ISBN 978-1-0980-9588-8 (digital)

Christian Faith Publishing, Inc.
832 Park Avenue
Meadville, PA 16335
www.christianfaithpublishing.com

Printed in the United States of America

Praises for
*Doing All the Good You Can Daily: 31 Days of
Phyllis' Success Predictors and Possibilities*

Phyllis Pottinger's *31 Days of Doing All the Good You Can* is a daily guide of simple practices that focuses on being intentional about one's life and the lives of others. Phyllis understands the importance of doing all the good she can to bring love and joy to others. She lives it. This is a must-read for anyone wanting to do the same.

—Judith John, Senior Sales Director

Our authors, Phyllis Pottinger and Camille Whitehorn, of the book *Doing All the Good You Can Daily: 31 Days of Phyllis' Success Predictors and Possibilities*, have given us a fascinating compilation. Based on the philosophy of Ms. Pottinger's mother, "Doing Good Daily," she has pulled together many of the precepts of her faith, which is Roman Catholic. With text taken from the New and Old Testaments of the Bible, traditional words of prayer, quotations from famous writers, lyrics from pop songs and traditional hymns, Ms. Pottinger has created a thirty-one-day guide that serves to inspire folks to "do all the good you can daily." This book can be very much a guide to live fully each day of the month to get us back on track each day by putting God first so that all we do in a day will be for the good of God, others, and ourselves, which, of course, is doing God's will!

—Deacon Allan Longo

As soon as you pick up this heartfelt journeyed text, it is evident that this author has lived the journey herself. The use of scripture in her own life has become a habitual aid in all she lives. By seeing the positive effects in her personal experiences, she has been able to share quite efficiently that love with us. She serves us a practical plan, which includes easily accomplished goals as long as the reader desires. These suggestions have the ability to give the "doer" ample satisfaction. It is a compendium of scripture, prayer, and hymnal brimming over with this author's enthusiasm. She uncommonly respects the fact that scripture is the inspired word of God. There are many "self-help" books available, but this is a "God-help" book because the author can easily testify how He has transformed her in powerful ways. You can almost hear and see this energetic author singing with you. She certainly got me singing. Now it's your turn. Blessing to all who partake.

—Ellen Lobasso Educator, Lecturer

In Memory of My Mother, Alma Todd

For as early as I can remember, I have had many thoughts of wonderful memories of my grandparents loving all of us grandchildren, loving family, relatives, friends, and neighbors, being friendly, caring, supportive, kind and doing a world of good always for others. Their values and way of life were passed on to their children, the next generation, my parents, who exemplified those values and lived them their entire lives on earth.

My siblings and I, the third generation of living lives of doing good, witnessed and observed our parents following in the footsteps of their parents and living out the gospel with words taken from Matthew 19:19, "honor your father and mother,' and 'love your neighbor as yourself," and from Hebrews 13:16 "And do not forget to do good and to share with others, for with such sacrifices God is pleased."

Learning from and observing our parents and seeing the love, honor, and respect they gave to their parents were a template for us in loving, respecting, honoring, and serving our parents, family, friends, relatives, loved ones, and neighbors.

My mother, a wonderful and beloved wife, mother, sister, grandmother, great-grandmother, great-great-grandmother, godmother, friend, and neighbor, loved to sing and was a world-class seamstress. She passionately loved her God, her family, her many relatives, her godchildren and, extended family. She had the most angelic voice and was a pillar in the community. It was very important to her that she was responsible in doing her part in some way to meet the needs of the church for years. Our home was a home for everyone.

My mother was very welcoming and hospitable. She created a safe haven for all. She would watch over the neighborhood children and nurture them until their parents returned from work. Mother treated everyone with love, respect, and dignity. She was always ready, willing, and prepared with a loving, kind, eager, and caring heart and hands to reach out to do good for the good of others. She gave humble service to others, spending precious and life-changing quality time with individuals young and old, male and female, and with families encouraging, educating, advising, and empowering them in home-based business, taking care of their families, and being a good neighbor.

She was a teacher, role model, and mentor to countless others. Many people who visited and spent time with Mother felt important and special as Mother was never rushing. She listened to them, discussed their situation, worked on plans for progress, then she would feed them. Mother always prepared meals more than what was needed for our family so that she would always be ready and prepared with a meal for anyone who stopped by. And yes, people always stopped by. No one ever left our home hungry. Yes, through her words and her delicious food she ministered, consoled, and comforted others. Mother truly lived the Golden Rule.

In conversations, my mother would say to all, "I love you. Be strong." In addition, she would always say to me, "Never render evil for evil no matter what." "Do all the good you can in all the ways you can to all the people you can for as long as you can." I would then repeat every word followed by making a promise to her that I would do good daily no matter what and that she could count on me—a promise that I've kept to this very day. Doing good daily is a way of life for us. It's a joy to follow in my Mother's footsteps and to honor her legacy with this book, *Doing All the Good You Can Daily: 31 Days of Phyllis' Success Predictors and Possibilities.*

I lovingly encourage individuals, families, and various groups to join in and commit to doing all the good you can in all the ways you can to all the people you can for as long as you can daily. It is our wish for all of our readers that as you do good daily, your life will be transformed and filled with joy, and you will play a role in transforming countless lives in your family, community, country, and the world. Let's keep in mind words from Galatians 6:9:

> Let us not become weary in doing good, for
> at the proper time we will reap a harvest if we do
> not give up.

That's living the commandments: love God and love one another.

Contents

Foreword

It is an honor to write this foreword for *Doing All the Good You Can Daily: 31 Days of Phyllis' Success Predictors and Possibilities* written by the inspirational Phyllis Pottinger. I intend to keep this brief because I am so excited to have you dive in and experience the blessings of this book yourself!

Phyllis has a gift for making the large and lofty goal of navigating this life with faith and grace an accessible one, one that we can experience now. Phyllis and her message have had a profound impact on my life. The practice of doing good daily has been a source of great peace and provided me with a simple way to make sure that every day is filled with purpose and meaning. I look forward to each day's suggested action and love how this gentle practice can create a better world.

Phyllis designed the book with room to add our favorite scriptures, insights, and prayers, making it a genuine companion on our life's journey. Phyllis believes in the potential we all possess to be a light for others in our unique way. This book is one we can reach for whenever we need some inspiration, solace, peace, and the reminder that we are never alone. Phyllis' Success Predictors and Possibilities offer daily guidance. They provide a beautiful balance of caring for self and others, creating abundance, and sharing it. It is fulfilling and exciting to see how these incremental steps build and grow over days, weeks, months, and years and improve lives!

Phyllis does indeed do good daily and has lived by and proven these 31 Days of Phyllis' Success Predictors and Possibilities. She has brought them to her many roles—from a dedicated volunteer, active parishioner, beloved friend, loving mother, grandmother, and great-grandmother to her leadership as a national sales director. This is her recipe for faith in action! To know Phyllis is to love and be inspired by her. I invite you to get to know her too. So let's turn the page and begin!

May God bless you always.

Jacqueline Demeri Costello, Catechist
September 5, 2020, Feast of Blessed Mother Teresa

Acknowledgements

Joyful thanks to my mother, father, stepfather, and grandparents for the privilege of being their daughter and granddaughter, learning from them, and following in their footsteps.

To my siblings, thank you for caring and for being supportive throughout the years.

Heartfelt and loving thanks to my son, Robert, and daughter, Tanya. Thanks be to God for gifting me with both of them. I am deeply grateful for their love, care, kindness, compassion, and doing good.

And to my beloved grandchildren: Camille, Kaitlin, Robert III, Deanna, Marcus, and Sydney and my joyous great-grandchildren Emerson (EJ) and Leylah, I love you all with all of my heart.

I am extremely thankful, prayerful, forever grateful, and appreciative to my granddaughter Camille. Her brilliance, gifts, talents, commitment, and hard work made this book possible. Camille researched, compiled, and prepared the manuscript. I am beholden to you, my marvelous granddaughter.

A world of thanks to Jacqueline Costello, author and instructor, who graciously guided, encouraged, and supported me from the embryonic stage of this book to its publication. Precious thanks for the beautiful words you shared in the foreword in the beginning of the book. I will follow your exemplary performance and write additional books.

Profound thanks to Judith John for her consistent and continued support for decades. Judith exemplifies sacred words from Philippians 2:4. Look out for one another's interests, not just your own. Everyone loves Judith and Judith loves everyone.

Affectionate thanks to Ellen Lobasso, a leader in our church's devotional life and community of faith programs and events. She's a devoted and tireless servant of God from whom I have learned a lot. Ellen's love, support, and generosity are without measure.

Prayerful thanks and gratitude to Deacon Allan Longo who, through his faithful and exemplary service, his remarkable teaching, preaching, and resonating homilies in addition to his advice, instruction and generosity, have contributed to my growth spiritually, always drawing me closer to serving God.

Prayerful thanks to family members, relatives, friends, business family, church family, neighbors, and acquaintances for your contribution to this book and my life and for doing good. Together, we will continue to do good. And when everyone owns a copy of the book, reads it, and does good daily, we will create a world of people doing good daily, and my mother's legacy will live on. You're a blessing, and I am grateful, joyful, and blessed with you in my life.

Introduction

The book of Genesis tells us that in the beginning, when God created the heavens and earth, the earth was a formless void, and darkness covered the face of the earth while a wind from God swept over the face of the waters. Then God said, "Let there be light," and there was light! God gave us this beautiful world. He gave us a microcosm of wonderment.

Doing All the Good You Can Daily: 31 Days of Phyllis' Success Predictors and Possibilities will guide you in making each day the quintessential BEST DAY ever! It is designed to help you reflect and act/do because it is imperative that we stop and take the time to appreciate, celebrate, share, care, live, love, and enjoy life, thanking the Lord for all he has done and is doing and all he has afforded us. Remember, Jesus calls us to love one another and to love our neighbor as ourselves.

As Mother Teresa once said, "It's not how much we give, but how much love we put into giving." We must attempt to be the greatest versions of ourselves at all times. By reaching out to others and doing good, we can make a world of difference in the lives of others, maybe someone who is struggling or someone who needs a word of encouragement or support. Oftentimes, we are so enthralled in our daily routine we fail to realize what is going on around us

We must keep in mind that our words and actions matter and will impact and improve lives. We each must be responsible, play our part, and be responsive to the needs of our neighbor, brother, and sister, and do our part to improve lives. Whether we donate to a cause or contribute our time, money, talent, gifts or a simple smile or say a prayer, these actions can be monumental for someone having a rough day or for someone knowing you're thinking about them. As Scottish author, Ian MacLaren, once said, "Be kind. Everyone you meet is carrying a heavy burden." Everyone is unique, special, important, and ought to be loved, respected and to be treated with dignity.

Use this book to lighten the load and lessen the burden for others. They have certainly lightened our load and lessened our burdens. We want you to experience the joy! Each day, choose one of the 31 Days of Phyllis' Success Predictors and Possibilities and put it into action. Watch your life and the lives of others transform right before your eyes, only exuding positivity and light. Say it loud, "Seize the moment today," and make it significant and memorable. Yes, you are a difference maker!

31 Days of Phyllis' Success Predictors and Possibilities

*Requires Daily Action

1. Reach out in kindness to a sister today.
2. Share your blessings with many today. Say it out loud, "I believe I can."
3. Be generous today with your time, talent, skills, and treasure—a great opportunity to be kind, to give and serve others.
4. Offer prayers for family, friends, loved ones, leaders, neighbors, and victims of the 2020 coronavirus pandemic and their families today.
5. Don't hoard your success. Share it with someone today. Encourage them to improve and grow.
6. Ask for help today—an opportunity to make progress.
7. Give to a charitable organization today. Give thanks for your many blessings.
8. Grow your group, team or partnership by enrolling one new person today.
9. Send a card/note today.
10. Write a note to Jesus, thanking Him for your beautiful life today.
11. Generate one-thousand-dollars worth of business today.
12. Buy something today.

13. Set an outrageous goal today.
14. Make a decision about something on your mind today.
15. Treat yourself to something you love today.
16. Spend time with a loved one today.
17. Volunteer for a cause today. Count your blessings.
18. Inspire someone today.
19. Pay it forward today. Love God and love one another. God is love.
20. Open a book and read a chapter or two today or open the bible and read the Beatitudes (Matthew 5:1–12) or other scriptures.
21. Carve out quiet time and be mindful of your thoughts today.
22. Be mindful of your goal and accelerate your actions today.
23. Put your faith in action today. Let Jesus' face shine on us.
24. Do four things that will improve your life today. "I can do all things through Christ who strengthens me."
25. Recite your favorite scripture verse and put it into action today.
26. Show your love to an acquaintance or stranger today. With respect, compassion, an open mind, and open heart, welcome, embrace, and celebrate diversity and differences. Let the Golden Rule be your motivation to treat others the way you want to be treated.
27. Light the way for others with your words today. Read Psalm 27.
28. Do something spectacular for someone today—a family member, a friend, a loved one or a neighbor.
29. Read, look at, and listen to something/someone motivational/ inspirational today.
30. Attend/participate in an event today. That will enhance, improve, and enrich your life, church, school, organization, and/or community.
31. Smile a lot today. Pray, sing, laugh, give thanks, maintain a positive attitude, and express gratitude and appreciation.

Lord Jesus, today and every day I will take the time to love someone with intention.

1.	Reach out in kindness to a sister today.	*Ecclesiastes 4:9–10* Two are better than one, because they have a good return for their labor: If either of them falls down, one can help the other up.
2.	Share your blessings with many today. Say it out loud, "I believe I can."	*Philippians 4:13* I can do all things through Christ who strengthens me.
3.	Be generous today with your time, talent, skills and treasure—a great opportunity to be kind, to give and serve others.	*2 Corinthians 9:6* Remember this: Whoever sows sparingly will also reap sparingly, and whoever sows generously will also reap generously.
4.	Offer prayers for family, friends, loved ones, leaders, neighbors, and victims of the 2020 coronavirus pandemic and their families today.	*1 Timothy 2:1–2* I urge you, first of all, to pray for all people. Ask God to help them; intercede on their behalf and give thanks for them. Pray this way for kings and all who are in authority so that we can live peaceful and quiet lives marked by godliness and dignity.
5.	Ask for help today—an opportunity to make progress.	*Matthew 6:33* But seek first his kingdom and his righteousness, and all these things will be given to you as well.

6.	Don't hoard your success. Share it with someone today. Encourage them to improve and grow.	*Matthew 7:7* "Ask, and it will be given to you; seek, and you will find; knock, and it will be opened to you." *2 Kings 2:9* When they came to the other side, Elijah said to Elisha, "Tell me what I can do for you before I am taken away." And Elisha replied, "Please let me inherit a double share of your spirit and become your successor."
7.	Give to a charitable organization today. Give thanks for your many blessings	*Psalms 7:17* "I will give to the Lord the thanks due to his righteousness, and I will sing praise to the name of the Lord, the Most High."
8.	Grow your group, team or partnership by enrolling one new person today.	*Luke 10:27* And he answered, "You shall love the Lord your God with all your heart and with all your soul and with all your strength and with all your mind, and your neighbor as yourself."

9. Send a card/note today to bring a touch of caring, celebration, elegance, and graciousness, healing and wellness to your life and the lives of others.	*1 John 4:7–8* "Dear friends, let us love one another, for love comes from God. Everyone who loves has been born of God and knows God. Whoever does not love does not know God, because God is love." *Proverbs 16:24* Kind words are like honey—sweet to the soul and healthy for the body.
10. Write a note to Jesus thanking Him for your beautiful life today and for His love, goodness, and mercy.	*Colossians 3:17* And whatever you do, in word or deed, do everything in the name of the Lord Jesus, giving thanks to God the Father through him.
11. Generate one-thousand-dollars worth of business today.	*Psalm 16:11* You make known to me the path of life; in your presence there is fullness of joy; at your right hand are pleasures forevermore.

12. Buy something today.	*Matthew 11:28–30* Come to me, all who labor and are heavy laden, and I will give you rest. Take my yoke upon you, and learn from me, for I am gentle and lowly in heart, and you will find rest for your souls. For my yoke is easy, and my burden is light." *Proverbs 23:23* Buy the truth and do not sell it-wisdom, instruction and insight as well.
13. Set an outrageous goal today.	*Psalm 33:11* "But the plans of the Lord stand firm forever, the purposes of his heart through all generations."
14. Make a decision about something on your mind today.	*Proverbs 16:3* "Commit to the Lord whatever you do, and he will establish your plans."
15. Treat yourself to something you love today.	*Song of Solomon 4:7* You are altogether beautiful, my love; there is no flaw in you.
16. Spend time with a loved one today.	*John 15:5* I am the vine; you are the branches. Whoever abides in me and I in him, he it is that bears much fruit, for apart from me you can do nothing.

17. Volunteer for a cause today. Count your blessings.	*Philippians 4:19* And my God will supply every need of yours according to his riches in glory in Christ Jesus.
18. Inspire someone today.	*Jeremiah 29:1* "For I know the plans I have for you," declares the LORD, "plans to prosper you and not to harm you, plans to give you hope and a future.
19. Pay it forward today. Love God and love one another. God is love.	*2 Corinthians 9:7* Each one must give as he has decided in his heart, not reluctantly or under compulsion, for God loves a cheerful giver.
20. Open a book and read a chapter or two today or open the bible and read the Beatitudes (Matthew 5:1–12) or other scriptures.	*Psalm 119:18* Open my eyes, that I may behold wondrous things out of your law.
21. Carve out quiet time and be mindful of your thoughts today. Be still. Silence is golden.	*Philippians 4:6–7* Do not be anxious about anything, but in everything by prayer and supplication with thanksgiving let your requests be made known to God. And the peace of God, which surpasses all understanding, will guard your hearts and your minds in Christ Jesus.

22. Be mindful of your goal and accelerate your actions today.	*Proverbs 4:23* Keep your heart with all vigilance, for from it flow the springs of life.
23. Put your faith in action today. Let Jesus' face shine on us.	*Matthew 21:22* And whatever you ask in prayer, you will receive, if you have faith
24. Do four things that will improve your life today. "I can do all things through Christ who strengthens me."	*Ecclesiastes 3:1* There is a time for everything, and a season for every activity under the heavens.
25. Recite your favorite scripture verse and put it into action today.	*Luke 11:9* And I tell you, ask, and it will be given to you; seek, and you will find; knock, and it will be opened to you.
26. Show your love to an acquaintance or stranger today. With respect, compassion, an open mind, and open heart, welcome, embrace and celebrate diversity and differences. Let the Golden Rule be your motivation to treat others the way you want to be treated.	*John 13:35* By this everyone will know that you are my disciples, if you love one another."
27. Light the way for others with your words today. Read Psalm 27	*Psalm 27*

28. Do something spectacular for someone today—a family member, a friend, a loved one or a neighbor.	*Romans 12:12* Be joyful in hope, patient in affliction, and faithful in prayer.
29. Read, look at, and listen to something/someone motivational/inspirational today.	*Proverbs 2:2* Making your ear attentive to wisdom and inclining your heart to understanding;
30. Attend/participate in an event today that will enhance, improve, and enrich your life, church, school, organization and/or community.	*Hebrews 13:16* Do not neglect to do good and to share what you have, for such sacrifices are pleasing to God.
31. Smile a lot today. Pray, sing, laugh, give thanks, maintain a positive attitude, and express gratitude and appreciation.	*Proverbs 31:25* Strength and dignity are her clothing, and she laughs at the time to come.

1.	Reach out in kindness to a sister today.	*Galatians 6:2* Bear one another's burdens, and so fulfill the law of Christ.
2.	Share your blessings with many today. Say it out loud, "I believe I can."	*Mark 9:23* Jesus said unto him, If thou canst believe, all things are possible to him that believeth.
3.	Be generous today.	*Proverbs 19:17* Whoever is kind to the poor lends to the LORD, and he will reward them for what they have done.
4.	Offer prayers for family and friends today.	*Acts 20:35* In everything I did, I showed you that by this kind of hard work we must help the weak, remembering the words the Lord Jesus himself said: "It is more blessed to give than to receive."
5.	Don't hoard your success. Share it with someone today.	*Kings 2:3* And observe what the LORD your God requires: Walk in obedience to him, and keep his decrees and commands, his laws and regulations, as written in the Law of Moses. Do this so that you may prosper in all you do and wherever you go

6. Ask for help today.	*1 John 1:9* If we confess our sins, he is faithful and just to forgive us our sins and to cleanse us from all unrighteousness.
7. Give to a charitable organization today. Give thanks for your many blessings	*Proverbs 18:16* A gift opens the way and ushers the giver into the presence of the great.
8. Grow your group, team or partnership by enrolling one new person today.	*John 1:7* But if we walk in the light, as he is in the light, we have fellowship with one another, and the blood of Jesus, his Son, purifies us from all sin.
9. Send a card/note today.	*Habakkuk 2:2* And the Lord answered me: "Write the vision; make it plain on tablets, so he may run who reads it.
10. Write a note to Jesus thanking Him for your beautiful life today.	*Jeremiah 30:2* Thus says the Lord, the God of Israel, 'Write all the words which I have spoken to you in a book.'
11. Generate one-thousand-dollars worth of business today.	*Proverbs 31:16* She considers a field and buys it; From her earnings she plants a vineyard.

12. Buy something today.	*Revelation 1:3* Blessed is he who reads and those who hear the words of the prophecy, and heed the things which are written in it; for the time is near.
13. Set an outrageous goal today.	*1 Thessalonians 4:18* 18 Therefore encourage one another with these words.
14. Make a decision about something on your mind today.	*Romans 12:2* Do not conform yourselves to the standards of this world, but let God transform you inwardly by a complete change of your mind. Then you will be able to know the will of God—what is good and is pleasing to him and is perfect.
15. Treat yourself to something you love today.	*Luke 12:32* Fear not, little flock; for it is your Father's good pleasure to give you the kingdom.
16. Spend time with a loved one today.	*Matthew 18:20* For where two or three gather in my name, there am I with them.
17. Volunteer for a cause today. Count your blessings.	*Proverbs 11:25* Whoever brings blessing will be enriched, and one who waters will himself be watered.

18. Inspire someone today.	*Psalm 34:8* Taste and see that the LORD is good; blessed is the one who takes refuge in him.
19. Pay it forward today.	*Luke 6:38* Give, and it will be given to you. A good measure, pressed down, shaken together and running over, will be poured into your lap. For with the measure you use, it will be measured to you.
20. Open a book and read a chapter or two today.	*Psalm 119:130* The unfolding of Your words gives light; It gives understanding to the simple.
21. Carve out quiet time and be mindful of your thoughts today.	*2 Timothy 1:7* For the Spirit God gave us does not make us timid, but gives us power, love and self-discipline.
22. Be mindful of your goal and accelerate your actions today.	*Psalm 20:4* May he give you the desire of your heart and make all your plans succeed.

23. Put your faith in action today.	*Matthew 17:20* He replied, "Because you have so little faith. Truly I tell you, if you have faith as small as a mustard seed, you can say to this mountain, 'Move from here to there,' and it will move. Nothing will be impossible for you."
24. Do four things that will improve your life today.	*James 1:22* But be ye doers of the word, and not hearers only, deceiving your own selves.
25. Recite your favorite scripture verse and put it into action today.	*Colossians 3:23–24* Whatever you do, work heartily, as for the Lord and not for men, knowing that from the Lord you will receive the inheritance as your reward. You are serving the Lord Christ.
26. Show your love to a stranger today.	*Joshua 1:9* Have I not commanded you? Be strong and courageous. Do not be afraid; do not be discouraged, for the Lord your God will be with you wherever you go.

27. Light the way for others with your words today. Read Psalm 27	*Psalm 27* Of David. The LORD is my light and my salvation—whom shall I fear? Though an army besiege me, my heart will not fear; though war break out against me, even then will I be confident.
28. Do something spectacular for your family today.	*1 Corinthians 13:13* So now faith, hope, and love abide, these three; but the greatest of these is love.
29. Read, look at, and listen to something/someone motivational/inspirational today.	*2 Timothy 2:2* And what you have heard from me in the presence of many witnesses entrust to faithful men who will be able to teach others also.
30. Attend/participate in an event today.	*Deuteronomy 31:6* Be strong and courageous. Do not be afraid or terrified because of them, for the LORD your God goes with you; he will never leave you nor forsake you.
31. Smile a lot today. Pray, pray, pray, give thanks, maintain a positive attitude, and express gratitude and appreciation.	*Philippians 4:6* Do not be anxious about anything, but in every situation, by prayer and petition, with thanksgiving, present your requests to God.

Inspiration

We all know Rosie the Riveter, the cultural icon of World War II. She represented the women who worked in factories and shipyards during the war, many of whom produced munitions and war supplies. These women sometimes took entirely new jobs, replacing the male workers who joined the military.

Rosie the Riveter is used as a symbol of American feminism and women's economic advantage. She inspired millions of women to dig down deep within and exemplify their inner strength during an extremely trying time. Be like Rosie the Riveter and show the world how tough you are! Do something to better humanity in your community, in your small corner of the world. Make things better, encourage, lead, energize, love, and provide insight to those around you.

The Bible tells us in the book of Timothy that:

> All Scripture is breathed out by God and profitable for teaching, for reproof, for correction, and for training in righteousness, that the man of God may be competent, equipped for every good work. (2 Timothy 3:16–17)

READY, SET, INSPIRE!

> I urge, then, first of all, that petitions, prayers, intercession and thanksgiving be made for everyone.
>
> —1 Timothy 2:1

Motivation

Jack Roosevelt Robinson was an American professional baseball player who became the first African American to play in Major League Baseball in the modern era. Robinson broke the baseball color barrier when the Brooklyn Dodgers started him at first base on April 15, 1947. When the Dodgers signed Robinson, they heralded the end of racial segregation in professional baseball that had relegated black players to the Negro leagues since the 1880s. Robinson was inducted into the Baseball Hall of Fame in 1962. Jackie Robinson was relentless and would not allow the racial bigotry and segregation to deter him from having his dreams come to fruition.

The book of Isaiah 40: 28–31 says:

> Have you not known? Have you not heard? The Lord is the everlasting God, the Creator of the ends of the earth. He does not faint or grow weary; his understanding is unsearchable. He gives power to the faint, and to him who has no might he increases strength. Even youths shall faint and be weary, and young men shall fall exhausted; but they who wait for the Lord shall renew their strength; they shall mount up with wings like eagles; they shall run and not be weary; they shall walk and not faint.

If we trust in the Lord and have faith, all things are possible. Jackie Robinson could have grown weary and given up hope, but he persevered. Strive for excellence, motivate others, and stay humble.

Reach Out

Suppose your local town councilman or councilwoman decided they would no longer represent your town's interests and support its people, who would reach out to us? Would we stay uninformed and in the dark?

In the book of Luke 10: 30–37, Jesus says:

> "A man was going down from Jerusalem to Jericho, when he was attacked by robbers. They stripped him of his clothes, beat him and went away, leaving him half dead. A priest happened to be going down the same road, and when he saw the man, he passed by on the other side. So too, a Levite, when he came to the place and saw him, passed by on the other side. But a Samaritan, as he traveled, came where the man was; and when he saw him, he took pity on him. He went to him and bandaged his wounds, pouring on oil and wine. Then he put the man on his own donkey, brought him to an inn and took care of him. The next day he took out two denarii[a] and gave them to the innkeeper. 'Look after him,' he said, 'and when I return, I will reimburse you for any extra expense you may have.'
>
> "Which of these three do you think was a neighbor to the man who fell into the hands of robbers?"

The expert in the law replied, "The one who had mercy on him."

Jesus told him, "Go and do likewise."

Reaching out is so important not only for you but for the other person as well. We can brighten someone's day by simply holding a door open or just by saying hello. We should strive to be like the good Samaritan in the book of Luke because we all need support sometimes. Be merciful as our Lord is merciful.

Phyllis' 31 Days: Corporal and Spiritual Works of Mercy

The Corporal and Spiritual Works of Mercy are actions we can perform that extend God's compassion and mercy to those in need. Combined with Phyllis' 31 Days of Success Predictors and Possibilities, you'll be well on your way to paying it forward exponentially.

Corporal Works of Mercy

The Corporal Works of Mercy are these kind acts by which we help our neighbors with their material and physical needs.

CORPORAL WORKS	31 DAYS (pertaining to Corporal Works)	SCRIPTURE
Feed the hungry	1. Reach out in kindness to a sister today. 2. Share your blessings with many today.	The generous will themselves be blessed, for they share their food with the poor. Proverbs 22:9

Shelter the homeless	17. Volunteer for a cause today. Count your blessings.	For I was hungry and you gave me something to eat, I was thirsty and you gave me something to drink, I was a stranger and you invited me in, Matthew 25:35
Clothe the naked	3. Be generous today.	I needed clothes and you clothed me, I was sick and you looked after me, I was in prison and you came to visit me. Matthew 25:36
Visit the sick and imprisoned	5. Don't hoard your success. Share it with someone today.	Yet if anyone suffers as a Christian, let him not be ashamed, but let him glorify God in that name. 1 Peter 4:16

Bury the dead	16. Spend time with a loved one today. 4. Offer prayers for family and friends today.	I would give my bread to the hungry and my clothing to the naked; and if I saw any one of my people dead and thrown out behind the wall of Nin'eveh, I would bury him. And if Sennach'erib the king put to death any who came fleeing from Judea, I buried them secretly. For in his anger he put many to death. When the bodies were sought by the king, they were not found. Then one of the men of Nin'eveh went and informed the king about me, that I was burying them; so I hid myself. When I learned that I was being searched for, to be put to death, I left home in fear. Tobit 1:17–19
Give alms to the poor	7. Give to a charitable organization today.	Then Jesus declared, "I am the bread of life. Whoever comes to me will never go hungry, and whoever believes in me will never be thirsty. John 6:35

Spiritual Works of Mercy

The Spiritual Works of Mercy are acts of compassion, as listed below, by which we help our neighbors with their emotional and spiritual needs.

SPIRITUAL WORKS	31 DAYS (pertaining to Spiritual Works)	SCRIPTURE
Instruct	23. Put your faith in action today.	Preach the word; be prepared in season and out of season; correct, rebuke and encourage—with great patience and careful instruction. 2 Timothy 4:2
Advise	26. Show your love to a stranger today.	Peace I leave with you; my peace I give you. I do not give to you as the world gives. Do not let your hearts be troubled and do not be afraid. John 14:27
Console	9. Send a card/note today.	However, as it is written: "What no eye has seen, what no ear has heard, and what no human mind has conceived" the things God has prepared for those who love him 1 Corinthians 2:9

Comfort	21. Carve out quiet time and be mindful of your thoughts today.	Be on your guard; stand firm in the faith; be courageous; be strong. Do everything in love. 1 Corinthians 16: 13–14
Forgive	25. Recite your favorite scripture verse and put it into action today. 31. Smile a lot today. Pray, pray, pray, give thanks, maintain a positive attitude and express gratitude and appreciation.	And when you stand praying, if you hold anything against anyone, forgive them, so that your Father in heaven may forgive you your sins." Mark 11:25
Bear wrongs patiently	27. Light the way for others with your words today. Read Psalm 27	So do not be ashamed of the testimony about our Lord or of me his prisoner. Rather, join with me in suffering for the gospel, by the power of God. 2 Timothy 1:8

Prayer

*P*atiently and profusely
*R*epentance and forgiveness
*A*doration and understanding
*Y*ield and listen, surrender to the Lord
*E*verlasting love
*R*ealizing how precious life is

Giving

*G*enerously
*I*mmersed in love
*V*oluntarily reaching out
*I*ncredibly selfless
*N*ever wavering from the Golden Rule
*G*ratitude

Love

*L*eading light
*O*pen-hearted
*V*irtuous
*E*mpowering

Power of Prayer

Task: Compose/develop your own personal prayer. Use it daily.

_____
_____
_____
_____
_____
_____
_____
_____
_____
_____
_____
_____
_____
_____
_____
_____
_____
_____

Use it to Pray Daily

Your participation in the 31 Days may touch your heart profoundly, prompting and empowering you to create your own personal daily prayer.

The Power of Prayer
Prayer changes things, so pray without ceasing.

P	Patiently and profusely	*2 Timothy 1:7* For the Spirit God gave us does not make us timid, but gives us power, love and self-discipline.
R	Repentance and forgiveness	*Ephesians 4: 31–32* Get rid of all bitterness, rage and anger, brawling and slander, along with every form of malice. Be kind and compassionate to one another, forgiving each other, just as in Christ God forgave you.
A	Adoration and understanding	*John 3:16* For God so loved the world, that he gave his only Son, that whoever believes in him should not perish but have eternal life.
Y	Yield and listen, surrender to the Lord	*1 John 1:9* If we confess our sins, he is faithful and just to forgive us our sins and to cleanse us from all unrighteousness.
E	Everlasting love	*Zephaniah 3:17* The Lord your God is in your midst, a mighty one who will save; he will rejoice over you with gladness; he will quiet you by his love; he will exult over you with loud singing
R	Realizing how precious life is	*Matthew 6:25* Therefore I tell you, do not be anxious about your life, what you will eat or what you will drink, nor about your body, what you will put on. Is not life more than food, and the body more than clothing?

Daily Prayer is important in order to keep a well-grounded and meaningful relationship with the Lord. It's easy for us to live our day-to-day lives with monotony not realizing how blessed and favored we truly are.

GIVING IS CARING: Give, and it will be given to you. A good measure, pressed down, shaken together and running over will be poured into your lap. For with the measure you use, it will be measured to you.

G	Generously	Luke 12:33 Sell your possessions and give to the poor. Provide purses for yourselves that will not wear out, a treasure in heaven that will never fail, where no thief comes near and no moth destroys.
I	Immersed in love	Isaiah 58:10 "Feed the hungry, and help those in trouble. Then your light will shine out from the darkness, and the darkness around you will be as bright as noon."
V	Voluntarily reaching out	Acts 20:35 "I have shown you in every way, by laboring like this, that you must support the weak. And remember the words of the Lord Jesus, that He said, 'It is more blessed to give than to receive."
I	Incredibly selfless	Luke 6:35 But love your enemies, and do good, and lend, expecting nothing in return, and your reward will be great, and you will be sons of the Most High, for he is kind to the ungrateful and the evil.
N	Never wavering from the Golden Rule	Colossians 3:23–24 Work willingly at whatever you do, as though you were working for the Lord rather than for people. Remember that the Lord will give you an inheritance as your reward, and that the Master you are serving is Christ. Matthew 7:12 So in everything, do to others what you would have them do to you, for this sums up the Law and the Prophets.
G	Gratitude	2 Corinthians 4:15 All this is for your benefit, so that the grace that is reaching more and more people may cause thanksgiving to overflow to the glory of God.

We should never turn a blind eye to the ailing or less fortunate because we never know what trials and tribulations they've been through. Empathy goes a long way.

Love is the Universal Language
Faith, hope, and love abide, but the greatest of all is love.

L	Leading light	Matthew 5:14–16 You are the light of the world. A city set on a hill cannot be hidden. Nor do people light a lamp and put it under a basket, but on a stand, and it gives light to all in the house. In the same way, let your light shine before others, so that[a]they may see your good works and give glory to your Father who is in heaven.
O	Open-hearted	Ephesians 1:18 Having the eyes of your hearts enlightened, that you may know what is the hope to which he has called you, what are the riches of his glorious inheritance in the saints.
V	Virtuous	2 Peter 1:5 For this very reason, make every effort to supplement your faith with virtue, [a] and virtue with knowledge.
E	Empowering	Deuteronomy 31:6 Be strong and courageous. Do not fear or be in dread of them, for it is the Lord your God who goes with you. He will not leave you or forsake you.

Words to Live By

Kindness

Praise be to the LORD, for he showed me the wonders of his love when I was in a city under siege. (*Psalm 31:21*)

Therefore, as God's chosen people, holy and dearly loved, clothe yourselves with compassion, kindness, humility, gentleness and patience. (*Colossians* 3:12)

Serve

Whoever serves me must follow me; and where I am, my servant also will be. My Father will honor the one who serves me. (*John 12:26*)

Joy

May the God of hope fill you with all joy and peace as you trust in him, so that you may overflow with hope by the power of the Holy Spirit. (*Romans 15:13*)

Zealous

Do not be slothful in zeal, be fervent in spirit, serve the Lord. (*Roman 12:11*)

Encourage

Those who sow in tears shall reap with shouts of joy! (*Psalm 126:5*)

May our Lord Jesus Christ himself and God our Father, who loved us and by his grace gave us eternal encouragement and good hope, encourage your hearts and strengthen you in every good deed and word. (*2 Thessalonians 2:16–17*)

Positive Attitude

And whatever you ask in prayer, you will receive, if you have faith. (*Matthew 21:12*)

Reach Out

And he answered, "You shall love the Lord your God with all your heart and with all your soul and with all your strength and with all your mind, and your neighbor as yourself." (*Luke 10:27*)

For the Son of Man came to seek and to save the lost. (*Luke 19:10*)

Peace

Casting all your anxieties on him, because he cares for you. (*1 Peter 5:7*)

Don't worry about anything; instead, pray about everything. Tell God what you need and thank him for all he has done. Then you will experience God's peace, which exceeds anything we can understand. His peace will guard your hearts and minds as you live in Christ Jesus. (*Philippians 4:6–7*)

Daily Prayers and Blessings

For flowers that bloom about our feet; For
tender grass so fresh and sweet; For song of
bird, and hum of bee; For all things fair we
hear or see, Father in heaven, we thank Thee!
—Ralph Waldo Emerson

This is the day the Lord has made; let us rejoice
and be glad. Give thanks to the Lord, for he
is good, for his mercy endures forever. Let the
house of Israel say, "His mercy endures forever."
"The right hand of the Lord has struck with
power; the right hand of the Lord is exalted." I
shall not die, but live, and declare the works of
the Lord." The stone which the builders rejected
has become the cornerstone. By the Lord has
this been done; it is wonderful in our eyes.
—Psalm 118

 Jesus, Others, You—Saint Mother Teresa

Prayer to Your Guardian Angel

Angel of God, my Guardian dear,
To whom God's love commits me here,
Ever this day be at my side,
To light and guard, to rule and guide. Amen.

God works for the Good of those who love him, who have been called according to his purpose.
—Romans 8:28

I urge you, brothers and sisters, by your lord Jesus Christ and by the love of the Spirit, to join me in my struggle by praying to God for me.
—Romans 15:30

Prayer to St. Jude
(Patron of Hopeless Causes)

Saint Jude, glorious apostle, faithful servant and friend of Jesus. The name of the traitor has caused you to be forgotten by many, but the true Church invokes you universally as the patron of things despaired of. Pray of me, who am so downcast. Pray of me, that finally I may receive the consolations and help of heaven in all my necessities, tribulations, and sufferings, particularly (make the request here), and that I may bless God with the elect throughout eternity. Amen.
Saint Jude, Apostle, martyr and relative of our Lord Jesus Christ of Mary, and of Joseph, interceded for us. Amen.

"Let him who boasts boast about this: that he understands and knows Me, that I am the Lord, who exercises kindness, justice and righteousness on earth, for in these I delight," declares the Lord.
—Jeremiah 9:24 (NIV)

In everything I did, I showed you that by this
kind of hard work we must help the weak,
remembering the words the Lord Jesus himself
said: 'It is more blessed to give than to receive.
—Acts 20:35

We Bear Fruits

3
ways

1. OUR ACTIONS: Enriching lives of others, bear good fruits, care.
2. OUR WORDS: Sirach—First formed in our minds, heart, then in our mouths. Praise thanksgiving, generosity, love. Use it for good. Encourage others.
3. OUR THOUGHTS: The way we treat others. Let our thoughts be rooted in clarity. Root out and evil fruits that we are bearing.

Praise our Lord always. Thank him. Use our
mouths to do this that we will bear good fruits.

Love is a fruit in season, and
within reach of every hand.
—Mother Teresa

Trees

Alfred Joyce Kilmer

I think that I shall never see
A poem lovely as a tree.

A tree whose hungry mouth is prest
Against the earth's sweet flowing breast;

A tree that looks at God all day,
And lifts her leafy arms to pray;

A tree that may in summer wear
A nest of robins in her hair;

Upon whose bosom snow has lain;
Who intimately lives with rain.

Poems are made by fools like me,
But only God can make a tree.

Phyllis' 31 Days of Success

Predictors and Possibilities

Gratitude
Journal

Gratitude List

Three Things You Are Grateful for Today:

1.

2.

3.

Gratitude List

Three Things You Are Grateful for Today:

1.

2.

3.

Taking Action Doing Good

Record your results of taking action and doing good daily:

1.

2.

3.

Taking Action Doing Good

Record your results of taking action & doing good daily:

1.

2.

3.

Reflections

Record your joy and gratitude of doing good daily.

_____
_____
_____
_____
_____
_____
_____
_____
_____
_____
_____
_____
_____
_____
_____
_____
_____
_____
_____
_____
_____
_____
_____
_____
_____
_____
_____
_____
_____

31 Days of Phyllis' Success Predictors and Possibilities

*Requires Daily Action
*Fill each box with your favorite scripture.

1. Reach out in kindness to a sister today.	
2. Share your blessings with many today. Say it out loud, "I believe I can."	
3. Be generous today.	
4. Offer prayers for family and friends today.	
5. Don't hoard your success. Share it with someone today.	
6. Ask for help today.	
7. Give to a charitable organization today. Give thanks for your many blessings	

8. Grow your group, team or partnership by enrolling one new person today.	
9. Send a card/note today.	
10. Write a note to Jesus, thanking Him for your beautiful life today.	
11. Generate one-thousand-dollars worth of business today.	
12. Buy something today.	
13. Set an outrageous goal today.	
14. Make a decision about something on your mind today.	
15. Treat yourself to something you love today.	
16. Spend time with a loved one today.	
17. Volunteer for a cause today. Count your blessings.	
18. Inspire someone today.	
19. Pay it forward today.	
20. Open a book and read a chapter or two today.	
21. Carve out quiet time and be mindful of your thoughts today.	

22. Be mindful of your goal and accelerate your actions today.	
23. Put your faith in action today.	
24. Do four things that will improve your life today.	
25. Recite your favorite scripture verse and put it into action today.	
26. Show your love to a stranger today.	
27. Light the way for others with your words today. Read Psalm 27	
28. Do something spectacular for your family today.	
29. Read, look, listen to something/someone motivational/inspirational today.	
30. Attend/participate in an event today.	
31. Smile a lot today. Pray, pray, pray, give thanks, maintain a positive attitude, and express gratitude and appreciation.	

A Reading from the Holy Gospel According to Matthew 6:1–6, 16–18

Jesus said to his disciples: Take care not to perform righteous deeds in order that people may see them; otherwise, you will have no recompense from your heavenly Father.

When you give alms, do not blow a trumpet before you, as the hypocrites do in the synagogues and in the streets to win the praise of others. Amen, I say to you, they have received their reward. But when you give alms, do not let your left hand know what your right is doing, so that your almsgiving may be secret. And your Father who sees in secret will repay you." When you pray, do not be like the hypocrites, who love to stand and pray in the synagogues and on street corners so that others may see them. Amen, I say to you, they have received their reward. But when you pray, go to your inner room, close the door, and pray to your Father in secret. And your Father who sees in secret will repay you. "When you fast, do not look gloomy like the hypocrites. They neglect their appearance, so that they may appear to others to be fasting. Amen, I say to you, they have received their reward. But when you fast, anoint your head and wash your face, so that you may not appear to others to be fasting, except to your Father who is hidden. And your Father who sees what is hidden will repay you."

A Reading from the Holy Gospel According to Matthew 5:43–48

Jesus said to his disciples: "You have heard that it was said, You shall love your neighbor and hate your enemy. But I say to you, love your enemies and pray for those who persecute you, that you may be children of your heavenly Father, for he makes his sun rise on the bad and the good and causes rain to fall on the just and the unjust. For if you love those who love you, what recompense will you have? Do not the tax collectors do the same? And if you greet your brothers only, what is unusual about that? Do not the pagans do the same? So be perfect, just as your heavenly Father is perfect."

The Beatitudes

Blessed are the poor in spirit,
for theirs is the kingdom of heaven.

Blessed are those who mourn, for they will be comforted.

Blessed are the meek, for they will inherit the earth.

Blessed are those who hunger and thirst for righteousness,
for they will be filled.

Blessed are the merciful, for they will be shown mercy.

Blessed are the pure in heart, for they will see God.

Blessed are the peacemakers,
for they will be called children of God.

Blessed are those who are persecuted because of righteousness,
for theirs is the kingdom of heaven.   Mathew 5:3-12

For we live by faith, not by sight. (2 Corinthians 5:7)

Love the Lord your God with all your heart and with all your soul and with all your mind and with all your strength. (Mark 12:30)

May the God of hope fill you with all joy and peace as you trust in him, so that you may overflow with hope by the power of the Holy Spirit. (Romans 15:13)

He will reply, "Truly I tell you, whatever you did not do for one of the least of these, you did not do for me." (Matthew 25:45)

Sovereign Lord, you are God! Your covenant is trustworthy, and you have promised these good things to your servant. (2 Samuel 7:28)

Matthew 25:31–46

The Sheep and the Goats

"When the Son of Man comes in his glory, and all the angels with him, he will sit on his glorious throne. All the nations will be gathered before him, and he will separate the people one from another as a shepherd separates the sheep from the goats. He will put the sheep on his right and the goats on his left.

"Then the King will say to those on his right, 'Come, you who are blessed by my Father; take your inheritance, the kingdom prepared for you since the creation of the world. For I was hungry and you gave me something to eat, I was thirsty and you gave me something to drink, I was a stranger and you invited me in, I needed clothes and you clothed me, I was sick and you looked after me, I was in prison and you came to visit me.'

"Then the righteous will answer him, 'Lord, when did we see you hungry and feed you, or thirsty and give you something to drink? When did we see you a stranger and invite you in, or needing clothes and clothe you? When did we see you sick or in prison and go to visit you?'

"The King will reply, 'Truly I tell you, whatever you did for one of the least of these brothers and sisters of mine, you did for me.'

"Then he will say to those on his left, 'Depart from me, you who are cursed, into the eternal fire prepared for the devil and his angels. For I was hungry and you gave me nothing to eat, I was thirsty and you gave me nothing to drink, I was a stranger and you did not invite me in, I needed clothes and you did not clothe me, I was sick and in prison and you did not look after me.'

"They also will answer, 'Lord, when did we see you hungry or thirsty or a stranger or needing clothes or sick or in prison, and did not help you?'

"He will reply, 'Truly I tell you, whatever you did not do for one of the least of these, you did not do for me.'

"Then they will go away to eternal punishment, but the righteous to eternal life."

As you go, proclaim the good news, "The kingdom of heaven has come near." Cure the sick, raise the dead, cleanse the lepers, cast out demons. You received without payment; give without payment. Take no gold, or silver, or copper in your belts, no bag for your journey, or two tunics, or sandals, or a staff; for laborers deserve their food. Whatever town or village you enter, find out who in it is worthy, and stay there until you leave. As you enter the house, greet it. If the house is worthy, let your peace come upon it; but if it is not worthy, let your peace return to you. If anyone will not welcome you or listen to your words, shake off the dust from your feet as you leave that house or town. Truly I tell you, it will be more tolerable for the land of Sodom and Gomorrah on the day of judgement than for that town.

—Matthew 10:7–15

with God,
ALL THINGS ARE POSSIBLE

Isaiah 58:6–11

Is not this the kind of fasting I have chosen:
to loose the chains of injustice
and untie the cords of the yoke,
to set the oppressed free
and break every yoke?
Is it not to share your food with the hungry
and to provide the poor wanderer with shelter—
when you see the naked, to clothe them,
and not to turn away from your own flesh and blood?
Then your light will break forth like the dawn,
and your healing will quickly appear;
then your righteousness[a] will go before you,
and the glory of the Lord will be your rear guard.
Then you will call, and the Lord will answer;
you will cry for help, and he will say: Here am I.
"If you do away with the yoke of oppression,
with the pointing finger and malicious talk,
and if you spend yourselves in behalf of the hungry
and satisfy the needs of the oppressed,
then your light will rise in the darkness,
and your night will become like the noonday.
The Lord will guide you always;
he will satisfy your needs in a sun-scorched land
and will strengthen your frame.
You will be like a well-watered garden,
like a spring whose waters never fail.

Psalm 23

A psalm of David

The Lord is my shepherd, I lack nothing.
He makes me lie down in green pastures,
he leads me beside quiet waters,
he refreshes my soul.
He guides me along the right paths
for his name's sake.
Even though I walk
through the darkest valley,
I will fear no evil,
for you are with me;
your rod and your staff,
they comfort me.

You prepare a table before me
in the presence of my enemies.
You anoint my head with oil;
my cup overflows.
Surely your goodness and love will follow me
all the days of my life,
And I will dwell in the house of the Lord forever.

Psalm 27

Of David.

The Lord is my light and my salvation—
whom shall I fear?
The Lord is the stronghold of my life—
of whom shall I be afraid?

When the wicked advance against me
to devour me it is my enemies and my foes
who will stumble and fall.
Though an army besiege me,
my heart will not fear;
though war break out against me,
even then I will be confident.

One thing I ask from the Lord,
this only do I seek:
that I may dwell in the house of the Lord
all the days of my life,
to gaze on the beauty of the Lord
and to seek him in his temple.
For in the day of trouble
he will keep me safe in his dwelling;
he will hide me in the shelter of his sacred tent
and set me high upon a rock.

Then my head will be exalted
above the enemies who surround me;
at his sacred tent I will sacrifice with shouts of joy;
I will sing and make music to the Lord.
Hear my voice when I call, Lord;
be merciful to me and answer me.
My heart says of you, "Seek his face!"
Your face, Lord, I will seek.

Do not hide your face from me,
do not turn your servant away in anger;
you have been my helper.
Do not reject me or forsake me,
God my Savior.
Though my father and mother forsake me,
the Lord will receive me.
Teach me your way, Lord;
lead me in a straight path
because of my oppressors.
Do not turn me over to the desire of my foes,
for false witnesses rise up against me,
spouting malicious accusations.

I remain confident of this:
I will see the goodness of the Lord
in the land of the living.
Wait for the Lord;
be strong and take heart
and wait for the Lord.

Psalm 35

Of David.

Contend, Lord, with those who contend with me;
fight against those who fight against me.
Take up shield and armor;
arise and come to my aid.
Brandish spear and javelin[a]
against those who pursue me.
Say to me,
"I am your salvation."
May those who seek my life
be disgraced and put to shame;
may those who plot my ruin
be turned back in dismay.
May they be like chaff before the wind,
with the angel of the Lord driving them away;
may their path be dark and slippery,
with the angel of the Lord pursuing them.
Since they hid their net for me without cause
and without cause dug a pit for me,
may ruin overtake them by surprise—
may the net they hid entangle them,
may they fall into the pit, to their ruin.
Then my soul will rejoice in the Lord
and delight in his salvation.
My whole being will exclaim,
"Who is like you, Lord?
You rescue the poor from those too strong for them,
the poor and needy from those who rob them."
Ruthless witnesses come forward;
they question me on things I know nothing about.
They repay me evil for good
and leave me like one bereaved.
Yet when they were ill, I put on sackcloth

and humbled myself with fasting.
When my prayers returned to me unanswered,
I went about mourning
as though for my friend or brother.
I bowed my head in grief
as though weeping for my mother.
But when I stumbled, they gathered in glee;
assailants gathered against me without my knowledge.
They slandered me without ceasing.
Like the ungodly they maliciously mocked;[b]
they gnashed their teeth at me.
How long, Lord, will you look on?
Rescue me from their ravages,
my precious life from these lions.
I will give you thanks in the great assembly;
among the throngs I will praise you.
Do not let those gloat over me
who are my enemies without cause;
do not let those who hate me without reason
maliciously wink the eye.
They do not speak peaceably,
but devise false accusations
against those who live quietly in the land.
They sneer at me and say, "Aha! Aha!
With our own eyes we have seen it."
Lord, you have seen this; do not be silent.
Do not be far from me, Lord.
Awake, and rise to my defense!
Contend for me, my God and Lord.
Vindicate me in your righteousness, Lord my God;
do not let them gloat over me.
Do not let them think, "Aha, just what we wanted!"
or say, "We have swallowed him up."
May all who gloat over my distress
be put to shame and confusion;
may all who exalt themselves over me

be clothed with shame and disgrace.
May those who delight in my vindication
shout for joy and gladness;
may they always say, "The Lord be exalted,
who delights in the well-being of his servant."
My tongue will proclaim your righteousness,
your praises all day long.

Psalm 40

Then I said, "Here I am, I have come—
it is written about me in the scroll.
I desire to do your will, my God;
your law is within my heart."

Psalm 40: 7–8

Do not cast me away when I am old;
do not forsake me when my strength is gone.

Psalm 91

Whoever dwells in the shelter of the Most High
will rest in the shadow of the Almighty.
I will say of the Lord, "He is my refuge and my fortress,
my God, in whom I trust."
Surely he will save you
from the fowler's snare
and from the deadly pestilence.
He will cover you with his feathers,
and under his wings you will find refuge;
his faithfulness will be your shield and rampart.
You will not fear the terror of night,
nor the arrow that flies by day,
nor the pestilence that stalks in the darkness,
nor the plague that destroys at midday.
A thousand may fall at your side,
ten thousand at your right hand,
but it will not come near you.
You will only observe with your eyes
and see the punishment of the wicked.
If you say, "The Lord is my refuge,"
and you make the Most High your dwelling,
no harm will overtake you,

no disaster will come near your tent.
For he will command his angels concerning you
to guard you in all your ways;
they will lift you up in their hands,
so that you will not strike your foot against a stone.
You will tread on the lion and the cobra;
you will trample the great lion and the serpent.
"Because he loves me," says the Lord, "I will rescue him;
I will protect him, for he acknowledges my name.
He will call on me, and I will answer him;
I will be with him in trouble,
I will deliver him and honor him.
With long life I will satisfy him
and show him my salvation."

Psalm 92

A psalm. A song. For the Sabbath day.

It is good to praise the Lord
and make music to your name, O Most High,
proclaiming your love in the morning
and your faithfulness at night,
to the music of the ten-stringed lyre
and the melody of the harp.
For you make me glad by your deeds, Lord;
I sing for joy at what your hands have done.
How great are your works, Lord,
how profound your thoughts!
Senseless people do not know,
fools do not understand,
that though the wicked spring up like grass
and all evildoers flourish,
they will be destroyed forever.
But you, Lord, are forever exalted.
For surely your enemies, Lord,
surely your enemies will perish;
all evildoers will be scattered.
You have exalted my horn[b] like that of a wild ox;
fine oils have been poured on me.
My eyes have seen the defeat of my adversaries;
my ears have heard the rout of my wicked foes.
The righteous will flourish like a palm tree,
they will grow like a cedar of Lebanon;
planted in the house of the Lord,
they will flourish in the courts of our God.
They will still bear fruit in old age,
they will stay fresh and green,
proclaiming, "The Lord is upright;
he is my Rock, and there is no wickedness in him."

Psalm 119:105–112

Your word is a lamp for my feet,
a light on my path.
I have taken an oath and confirmed it,
that I will follow your righteous laws.
I have suffered much;
preserve my life, Lord, according to your word.
Accept, Lord, the willing praise of my mouth,
and teach me your laws.
Though I constantly take my life in my hands,
I will not forget your law.
The wicked have set a snare for me,
but I have not strayed from your precepts.
Your statutes are my heritage forever;
they are the joy of my heart.
My heart is set on keeping your decrees
to the very end.

Hymns and Songs

I Will Follow Him

Love him, I love him, I love him
And where he goes I'll follow, I'll follow, I'll follow

I will follow him, follow him wherever he may go
There isn't an ocean too deep
A mountain so high it can keep me away

I must follow him (follow him), ever since he touched my hand I knew
That near him I always must be
And nothing can keep him from me
He is my destiny (destiny)

I love him, I love him, I love him
And where he goes I'll follow, I'll follow, I'll follow
He'll always be my true love, my true love, my true love
From now until forever, forever, forever

I will follow him (follow him), follow him wherever he may go
There isn't an ocean too deep
A mountain so high it can keep, keep me away
Away from my love (I love him, I love him, I love him)

I love him, I love him, I love him
And where he goes I'll follow, I'll follow, I'll follow
He'll always be my true love, my true love, my true love
From now until forever, forever, forever

I will follow him (follow him), follow him wherever he may go
There isn't an ocean too deep
A mountain so high it can keep, keep me away
Away from my love

And where he goes I'll follow, I'll follow, I'll follow
I know I'll always love him, I love him, I love him
And where he goes I'll follow, I'll follow, I'll follow
I know I'll always love him, I love him, I love him.

Great Is Thy Faithfulness

"Great is Thy faithfulness, "O God my Father,
There is no shadow of turning with Thee;
Thou changest not, Thy compassions, they fail not
As Thou hast been Thou forever wilt be.
"Great is Thy faithfulness!" "Great is Thy faithfulness!"
Morning by morning new mercies I see;
All I have needed Thy hand hath provided—
"Great is Thy faithfulness, "Lord, unto me!
Summer and winter, and springtime and harvest,
Sun, moon and stars in their courses above,
Join with all nature in manifold witness
To Thy great faithfulness, mercy and love.

"Great is Thy faithfulness!" "Great is Thy faithfulness!"
Morning by morning new mercies I see;
All I have needed Thy hand hath provided—
"Great is Thy faithfulness, "Lord, unto me!

Pardon for sin and a peace that endureth,
Thine own dear presence to cheer and to guide;
Strength for today and bright hope for tomorrow,
Blessings all mine, with ten thousand beside!

"Great is Thy faithfulness!" "Great is Thy faithfulness!"
Morning by morning new mercies I see;
All I have needed Thy hand hath provided—
"Great is Thy faithfulness, "Lord, unto me!"

This Little Light of Mine

This little light of mine
I'm gonna let it shine
This little light of mine
I'm gonna let it shine
This little light of mine
I'm gonna let it shine
Let it shine, let it shine, let it shine

This little light of mine
I'm gonna let it shine
This little light of mine
I'm gonna let it shine
This little light of mine
I'm gonna let it shine
Let it shine, let it shine, let it shine

For you and me
Let it shine for you and me
I'm gonna let it shine
Let it shine for you and me
I'm gonna let it shine
Let it shine for you and me
I'm gonna let it shine
Let it shine, let it shine, let it shine

For you and me
Let it shine for you and me
I'm gonna let it shine
Let it shine for you and me
I'm gonna let it shine
Let it shine for you and me
I'm gonna let it shine
Let it shine, let it shine.

Amazing Grace

Amazing grace, How sweet the sound
That saved a wretch like me.
I once was lost, but now I am found,
Was blind, but now I see.

'Twas grace that taught my heart to fear,
And grace my fears relieved.
How precious did that grace appear
The hour I first believed.

Through many dangers, toils and snares
I have already come,
'Tis grace has brought me safe thus far
And grace will lead me home.

The Lord has promised good to me
His word my hope secures;
He will my shield and portion be,
As long as life endures.

When we've been there ten thousand years
Bright shining as the sun,
We've no less days to sing God's praise
Than when we've first begun.

Amazing grace, How sweet the sound
That saved a wretch like me.
I once was lost, but now I am found,
Was blind, but now I see.

Here I Am, Lord

I, the Lord of sea and sky
I have heard my people cry
All who dwell in dark and sin
My hand will save
I who made the stars of night
I will make their darkness bright
Who will bear my light to them?
Whom shall I send?

Here I am, Lord
Is it I, Lord?
I have heard You calling in the night
I will go, Lord
If You lead me
I will hold Your people in my heart

I, the Lord of wind and flame
I will tend the poor and lame
I will set a feast for them
My hand will save
Finest bread I will provide
'Til their hearts be satisfied
I will give my life to them
Whom shall I send?

Here I am, Lord
Is it I, Lord?
I have heard You calling in the night
I will go, Lord
If You lead me
I will hold Your people in my heart
I will hold Your people in my heart

Be Not Afraid

You shall cross the barren desert
But you shall not die of thirst
You shall wander far in safety
Though you do not know the way
You shall speak your words to foreign men
And they will understand
You shall see the face of God and live

Be not afraid
I go before you always
Come, follow me and I will give you rest

If you pass through raging waters in the sea
You shall not drown
If you walk amid the burning flames
You shall not be harmed
If you stand before the power of hell
And death is at your side
Know that I am with you through it all

Be not afraid
I go before you always
Come, follow me and I will give you rest

And blessed are your poor
For the kingdom shall be theirs
Blest are you that weep and mourn
For one day you shall laugh
And if wicked men insult and hate you
All because of me
Blessed, blessed are you

Be not afraid
I go before you always
Come, follow me and I will give you rest

On Eagle's Wings

You who dwell in the shelter of the Lord
Who abide in His shadow for life
Say to the Lord, "My refuge, my rock in whom I trust!"

And He will raise you up on eagles' wings
Bear you on the breath of dawn
Make you to shine like the sun
And hold you in the palm of His hand

The snare of the fowler will never capture you
And famine will bring you no fear
Under His wings your refuge, His faithfulness your shield

And He will raise you up on eagles' wings
Bear you on the breath of dawn
Make you to shine like the sun
And hold you in the palm of His hand

You need not fear the terror of the night
Nor the arrow that flies by day
Though thousands fall about you, near you it shall not come

And He will raise you up on eagles' wings
Bear you on the breath of dawn
Make you to shine like the sun
And hold you in the palm of His hand

For to His angels He's given a command
To guard you in all of your ways
Upon their hands they will bear you up
Lest you dash your foot against a stone

And He will raise you up on eagles' wings
Bear you on the breath of dawn
Make you to shine like the sun
And hold you in the palm of His hand

And hold you, hold you in the palm of His hand.

I Surrender All

All to Jesus I surrender
All to Him I freely give
I will ever love and trust Him
In His presence daily live

All to Jesus I surrender
Humbly at His feet I bow
Worldly pleasures all forsaken
Take me Jesus take me now

I surrender all
I surrender all
All to Thee my blessed Saviour
I surrender all

All to Jesus I surrender
Make me Saviour wholly Thine
Let me feel the Holy Spirit
Truly know that Thou art mine

All to Jesus I surrender
Lord I give myself to Thee
Fill me with Thy love and power
Let Thy blessings fall on me

All to Jesus I surrender
Now I feel the sacred flame
Oh the joy of full salvation
Glory, glory to His name.

The Impossible Dream

To dream the impossible dream
To fight the unbeatable foe
To bear with unbearable sorrow
To run where the brave dare not go

To right the unrightable wrong
To love pure and chaste from afar
To try when your arms are too weary
To reach the unreachable star

This is my quest, to follow that star
No matter how hopeless, no matter how far
To fight for the right
Without question or pause
To be willing to march
Into hell for a heavenly cause

And I know if I'll only be true
To this glorious quest
That my heart will lay peaceful and calm
When I'm laid to my rest

And the world will be better for this
That one man scorned and covered with scars
Still strove with his last ounce of courage
To fight the unbeatable foe
To reach the unreachable star.

Reach Out and Touch (Somebody's Hand)

Reach out and touch
Somebody's hand
Make this world a better place
If you can
Reach out and touch
Somebody's hand
Make this world a better place
If you can

Take a little time out your busy day
To give encouragement
To someone who's lost the way
(Just try)
Or would I be talking to a stone
If I asked you
To share a problem that's not your own
(Oh no)
We can change things if we start giving
Why don't you

Reach out and touch
Somebody's hand
Make this world a better place
If you can
Reach out and touch
Somebody's hand
Make this world a better place
If you can

If you see an old friend on the street
And he's down
Remember his shoes could fit your feet
(Just try)
Try a little kindness and you'll see

It's something that comes
Very naturally
(Oh yeah)
We can change things if we…

We can change things if we start giving

Why don't you
(Why don't you)
Reach out and touch

Somebody's hand

Reach out and touch (reach out)
Somebody's hand
Make this world a better place
If you can
Reach out and touch
Somebody's hand (touch somebody's hand)
Make this world a better place If you can (why don't you)

Reach out and touch
Somebody's hand (somebody's hand)
Make this world a better place
If you can

Rock of Ages, Cleft for Me

Let me hide myself in thee;
Let the water and the blood,
From thy wounded side which flowed,
Be of sin the double cure,
Save from wrath and make me pure.

Not the labors of my hands
Can fill all thy law's demands;
Could my zeal no respite know,
Could my tears forever flow,
All for sin could not atone;
Thou must save, and thou alone.

While I draw this fleeting breath,
When mine eyes shall close in death,
When I rise to worlds unknown
And behold thee on thy throne,
Rock of Ages, cleft for me,
Let me hide myself in thee.

How Great Thou Art

O Lord, my God, when I in awesome wonder
Consider all the worlds Thy Hands have made
I see the stars, I hear the rolling thunder
Thy power throughout the universe displayed

Then sings my soul, my Saviour God, to Thee
How great Thou art, how great Thou art
Then sings my soul, my Saviour God, to Thee
How great Thou art, how great Thou art

And when I think of God, His Son not sparing
Sent Him to die, I scarce can take it in
That on the Cross, my burden gladly bearing
He bled and died to take away my sin

Then sings my soul, my Saviour God, to Thee
How great Thou art, how great Thou art
Then sings my soul, my Saviour God, to Thee
How great Thou art, how great Thou art

When Christ shall come with shout of acclamation
And lead me home, what joy shall fill my heart
Then I shall bow with humble adoration
And then proclaim, my God, how great Thou art

Then sings my soul, my Saviour God, to Thee
How great Thou art, how great Thou art
Then sings my soul, my Saviour God, to Thee
How great Thou art, how great Thou art.

God Is Standing By

When you have troubles don't cry
Just remember that God is standing by
Thank you, Lord

When you have heartaches
Don't cry, no, no, no, no, no
Don't worry, don't be discouraged
Don't cry, yeah
And sometime after sing

Oh, I'll be standing by
(That's what He told me, yeah)
So, I say there's no need to cry
Thank you Lord, yeah

Oh, I'll be standing by
(I'm gonna be standing, standing by, yeah)
So you see that there's no, no need to cry, yeah, yeah

I'd like to say one more thing
When you have heartaches you wonder why, yeah, yeah
But just remember, I want you to remember He's standing by
And you don't really have to worry about it, now

When you have trouble please
Don't cry, don't cry, don't cry oh, no, no, no
Don't worry, don't ever be discouraged
I want you to know you don't have to cry
And sometimes when your burdens get you down

But oh, I'll be standing by
(I'm gonna be standing by, thank you Lord, I thank you for seeing me)
So I get and no need, no need to cry

But oh, oh, I'll be standing by
(I'm gonna be standing by, thank you father, yeah, yeah)
So don't you worry and don't cry, yeah, don't cry, don't cry

No don't cry
No don't cry
No don't cry

Give Thanks with a Grateful Heart

Give thanks with a grateful heart
Give thanks to the Holy One
Give thanks because He's given Jesus Christ, His Son

Give thanks with a grateful heart
Give thanks to the Holy One
Give thanks because He's given Jesus Christ, His Son

And now let the weak say, "I am strong"
Let the poor say, "I am rich
Because of what the Lord has done for us"

And now let the weak say, "I am strong"
Let the poor say, "I am rich
Because of what the Lord has done for us"

Give thanks with a grateful heart (with a grateful heart)
Give thanks to the Holy One (to the Holy One)
Give thanks because He's given Jesus Christ, His Son

Give thanks with a grateful heart (with a grateful heart)
Give thanks to the Holy One (to the Holy One)
Give thanks because He's given Jesus Christ, His Son

And now let the weak say, "I am strong"
Let the poor say, "I am rich
Because of what the Lord has done for us"

And now let the weak say, "I am strong"
Let the poor say, "I am rich (I am rich)
Because of what the Lord has done for us"
Give thanks

We give thanks to You

Daily Prayers

The Lord's Prayer

Our Father, who art in heaven,
hallowed be thy Name,
thy kingdom come,
thy will be done,
on earth as it is in heaven.

Give us this day our daily bread.
And forgive us our trespasses,
as we forgive those
who trespass against us.

And lead us not into temptation,
but deliver us from evil.

For thine is the kingdom,
and the power, and the glory,
for ever and ever. Amen.

Pray continually, give thanks in
all circumstances; for this is God's
will for you in Christ Jesus.
—1 Thessalonians 5:17–18

Hail Mary, Full of Grace, The Lord is with thee. Blessed art thou among women, and blessed is the fruit of thy womb, Jesus. Holy Mary, Mother of God, pray for us sinners now, and at the hour of our death.

I thank God, whom I serve, as my ancestors
did, with a clear conscience, as night and day
I constantly remember you in my prayers.
Recalling your tears, I long to see you, so that
I may be filled with joy. I am reminded of
your sincere faith, which first lived in your
grandmother Lois and in your mother Eunice
and, I am persuaded, now lives in you also.
—2 Timothy 1:3–5

But the fruit of the Spirit is love, joy,
peace, forbearance, kindness, goodness,
faithfulness, gentleness and self-control.
Against such things there is no law.
—Galatians 5:22–23

Prayer of Saint Francis of Assisi

Lord, make me an instrument of your peace.
Where there is hatred, let me sow love;
Where there is injury, pardon;
Where there is doubt, faith;
Where there is despair, hope;
Where there is darkness, light;
Where there is sadness, joy.

O Divine Master, grant that I may not so much seek
To be consoled as to console;
To be understood as to understand;
To be loved as to love.
For it is in giving that we receive;
It is in pardoning that we are pardoned;
And it is in dying that we are born to eternal life.
Amen.

HOW TO SAY THE ROSARY

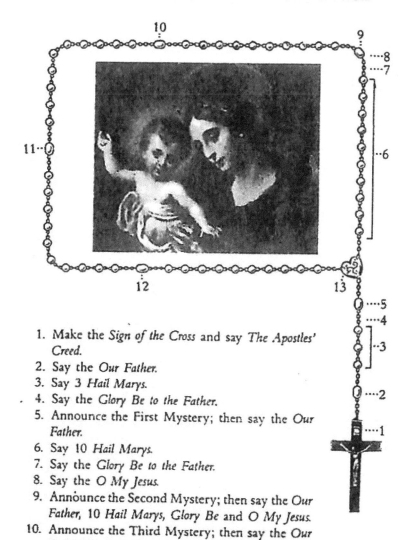

1. Make the *Sign of the Cross* and say *The Apostles' Creed.*
2. Say the *Our Father.*
3. Say 3 *Hail Marys.*
4. Say the *Glory Be to the Father.*
5. Announce the First Mystery; then say the *Our Father.*
6. Say 10 *Hail Marys.*
7. Say the *Glory Be to the Father.*
8. Say the *O My Jesus.*
9. Announce the Second Mystery; then say the *Our Father,* 10 *Hail Marys, Glory Be* and *O My Jesus.*
10. Announce the Third Mystery; then say the *Our Father,* 10 *Hail Marys, Glory Be* and *O My Jesus.*
11. Announce the Fourth Mystery; then say the *Our Father,* 10 *Hail Marys, Glory Be* and *O My Jesus.*
12. Announce the Fifth Mystery; then say the *Our Father,* 10 *Hail Marys, Glory Be* and *O My Jesus.*
13. Conclude by saying the *Hail, Holy Queen.*

THE MYSTERIES OF THE ROSARY

The Joyful Mysteries
Mondays and Saturdays
1. The Annunciation
2. The Visitation
3. The Birth of Jesus
4. The Presentation in the Temple
5. The Finding of Jesus in the Temple

The Sorrowful Mysteries
Tuesdays and Fridays
1. The Agony in the Garden
2. The Scourging at the Pillar
3. The Crowning with Thorns
4. The Carrying of the Cross
5. The Crucifixion

The Glorious Mysteries
Wednesdays and Sundays
1. The Resurrection of Jesus
2. The Ascension of Jesus
3. The Descent of the Holy Spirit
4. The Assumption of Mary
5. The Coronation of Mary

The Luminous Mysteries
Thursdays
1. The Baptism of Jesus
2. The Wedding at Cana
3. Jesus Proclaims the Kingdom
4. The Transfiguration
5. Jesus Institutes the Eucharist

The Apostles' Creed

I BELIEVE in God, the Father Almighty, Creator of heaven and earth; and in Jesus Christ, His only Son, our Lord; who was conceived by the Holy Ghost, born of the Virgin Mary, suffered under Pontius Pilate, was crucified, died, and was buried. He descended into Hell; the third day He arose again from the dead; He ascended into Heaven, sitteth at the right hand of God, the Father Almighty; from thence He shall come to judge the living and the dead. * I believe in the Holy Ghost, the Holy Catholic Church, the Communion of Saints, the forgiveness of sins, the resurrection of the body, and life everlasting. Amen.

Our Father

OUR FATHER, Who art in Heaven, hallowed be Thy Name. Thy kingdom come, Thy will be done on earth as it is in Heaven. * Give us this day our daily bread, and forgive us our trespasses, as we forgive those who trespass against us. And lead us not into temptation, but deliver us from evil. Amen.

Hail Mary

HAIL MARY, full of grace, the Lord is with thee; blessed art thou among women, and blessed is the Fruit of thy womb, Jesus. * Holy Mary, Mother of God, pray for us sinners, now and at the hour of our death. Amen.

Glory Be

GLORY BE to the Father, and to the Son, and to the Holy Ghost. * As it was in the beginning, is now, and ever shall be, world without end. Amen.

O My Jesus

To be said after the Glory Be to the Father following each decade of the Rosary. All pray it together.

O MY JESUS, forgive us our sins, save us from the fires of Hell, lead all souls to Heaven, especially those who are in most need of Thy mercy.

Hail, Holy Queen

HAIL, holy Queen, Mother of mercy, our life, our sweetness and our hope. To thee do we cry, poor banished children of Eve. To thee do we send up our sighs, mourning and weeping in this valley of tears. Turn then, most gracious advocate, thine eyes of mercy towards us. And after this our exile, show unto us the blessed Fruit of thy womb, Jesus. O clement, O loving, O sweet Virgin Mary.

V. Pray for us, O holy Mother of God.
R. That we may be made worthy of the promises of Christ.

Note: When the Rosary is said aloud by two or more persons, one person is the leader; he says the first part of each prayer, and everyone else answers by saying the remainder of the prayer (designated here by an asterisk). The *O My Jesus* and the body of the *Hail, Holy Queen* are said by all together.

Doing All the Good You Can Daily
31 Days of Phyllis' Success Predictors and Possibilities

Doing All the Good You Can Daily: 31 Days of Phyllis' Success Predictors and Possibilities is the ultimate life-changing and impactful book. It will not only inspire you, but it will also awaken your senses, open your hearts your minds, and invite all things good and positive into your life.

Designed by Phyllis Pottinger, an educator, entrepreneur, business leader, and inspirational speaker, this book can be worked by individuals, families and groups, bridging the gap and building intergenerational relationships. Delve into this book wholeheartedly and stimulate your spirit to doing what the Lord has called all of us to do.

The book includes a Gratitude Journal and space for you to jot down your experiences, thoughts, and more.

One reader has even said the book is "a beautiful maxim, yet often in these busy times, it can be a challenge to discern where to begin each day. So many important things seem to be competing for our time and attention! *Doing All the Good You Can Daily: 31 Days of Phyllis' Success Predictors and Possibilities* offers daily guidance."

In the same way, let your light shine before
others, so that they may see your good works
and give glory to your Father who is in heaven.
—Matthew 5:16

I am the vine; you are the branches. If you
remain in me and I in you, you will bear much
fruit; apart from me you can do nothing.
—John 15:5

About the Authors

Phyllis Pottinger is an educator, entrepreneur, business leader, inspirational speaker, and past president of the Parent-Teachers-Students Association (PTSA) in her school district. She's very involved in activities in her church. Phyllis is a Vincentian Volunteer of the Society of St. Vincent de Paul, an international organization. She plans and leads pilgrimages. She is a Marian Helper, a Marian Missionary of Divine Mercy, and an EWTN Media Missionary.

Phyllis lives the Golden Rule, strives, and thrives in doing good daily for the love of God, love of family, love of neighbor, and love of one another. Phyllis' never-ending love for her beloved mother, Miss Alma, who is resting with the Lord, propelled her to honor her mother for the way she lived her life—doing good daily.

Phyllis is blessed and gifted by God with her two beloved adult children: Robert and Tanya and their families. She follows in her mother's footsteps, zealously growing her legacy of doing good daily and leading by example.

Camille Whitehorn is the first grandchild of author Phyllis Pottinger. Camille is the daughter of Robert and Carol Whitehorn, sister to Kaitlin and Robert III, and mother to her precocious son Emerson Joseph. She is a firm believer in the *Doing All the Good You Can Daily: 31 Days of Phyllis' Success Predictors and Possibilities.*

With a Bachelor's of Science in both Biology as well as Clinical Laboratory Science. Camille credits her grandmother (Phyllis) for always instilling positivity and light into her life. Camille hopes this book touches the lives of many and makes a significant difference for all as it has done for her. She will always remember the words of her late great grandmother (Phyllis' Mother), "Stay strong," and her reminder to do good daily.

CPSIA information can be obtained
at www.ICGtesting.com
Printed in the USA
BVHW022040280122
627313BV00003B/167